Blockchain

Blockchain
Cryptocurrency, NFTs & Smart Contracts

**An executive guide to the world of
decentralized finance
2nd Edition**

Shelly Palmer

Shelly Palmer Digital Living Series
DIGITAL LIVING PRESS
www.shellypalmer.com

Published by Digital Living Press
2nd Edition, September 2021
1st Edition, May 2021

Digital Living Press
PO Box 1455, New York, NY 10156-1455
+1 (212) 532-3880

Copy Editor: Ellen Lohman
Editorial Assistant: Joey Lewandowski

For my wife, Debbie.

Table of Contents

Resources 9

Introduction 11

Blockchain aka Distributed Ledgers 11

Smart Contracts 16

The Key Question 18

Gas Prices (The Cost of Mining) 19

Layer 2: The Evolution of Blockchain Tech 20

Decentralization 22

Cryptocurrencies 24

Crypto Exchanges 24

Centralized DeFi: an oxymoron 26

Digital Wallets 26

Encrypting Your Crypto 26

Non-Fungible Tokens (NFTs) 32

When Will Crypto Be Useful? 39

Web 3.0 Things You Should Know 44

More Great Use Cases for Blockchain 49

How Crypto-Mining Works 52

What Is Encryption? 57

ICOs: What You Need to Know 60

The Philosophical Side of DeFi 63

Tales from under the Merkle Tree 66

The Creator Class & NFTs 70

Nuber: The End of Uber and Central Authority 74

Background Checks: Blockchain Can Help 77

Why Governments Fear Crypto 79

Porn Leads Tech, Again 84

Crypto: Parlor Trick or Paradigm Shift? 88

Conclusion 94

Blockchain Glossary 95

About The Author 114

Resources

The blockchain ecosystem is evolving rapidly.

For the latest information and useful links to the decentralized ecosystem (Crypto, NFTs, DeFi, DEX, Blockchain), please visit:

shellypalmer.com/blockchain

Links

Links referenced in this book can be found at:

shellypalmer.com/blockchain-book-links

Introduction

Crypto prices and NFTs are hogging the headlines, but they are just the most visible components of a rapidly growing decentralized financial system (DeFi) that has the potential to significantly challenge how we buy, sell, and trade just about everything. Blockchain and cryptocurrency may seem new, but they have been around for more than 10 years. The problem is that the world of crypto can be very confusing with all of its jargon, acronyms, and other unfamiliar words. This brief overview will introduce you to the basics.

Blockchain - aka Distributed Ledgers

A Blockchain Is Like Information Written in Stone

Carving a writing into a stone feels permanent. (Some writings in stone have lasted for millennia.) You can easily tell if a writing carved in stone has been altered and, maybe most importantly, the stone does not care what you carve (write) on it.

A blockchain shares these properties. You can think of a block on a blockchain as a digital stone. Blockchains live on a self-healing network distributed over a large number of computers. A blockchain is, for all intents and purposes, permanent. You can easily tell if the information has been altered, and blockchains do not care what information you add to them.

Blockchain Defined

A blockchain, or distributed ledger, is a continuously growing list (digital file) of encrypted transactions called "blocks" that are distributed (copied) to a peer-to-peer (P2P) network of computers.

Blocks

As described above, a blockchain is an immutable, sequential chain of records known as blocks. A block may contain any type of data, such as unique digital identifiers of physical products. Blocks are "chained" together by incorporating cryptographic hash functions ("hash"). In addition to user data, each block will contain an index, a timestamp, a list of transactions, a proof, and the hash of the previous block.

The Cryptographic Hash Function

A typical cryptographic hash function is a mathematical function that takes inputs of variable lengths to return outputs of a fixed length. The hash plays a critical role. Because each new block will contain a hash from the previous block, blockchains are immutable. If a hacker were to corrupt an earlier block in the blockchain, all subsequent blocks would contain incorrect hashes. There is an exceptional video from 3Blue1Brown on YouTube that beautifully explains the math behind cryptocurrencies and how bitcoins are stored on a blockchain: But how does bitcoin actually work? It is 26 minutes well spent. *[See Link 1 - shellypalmer.com/blockchain-book-links]*

Encrypted Transactions

Encrypted transactions (using conventional public/private key cryptography) are also key to blockchain's value. The user's "public key" is stored in a block and becomes an "address" on the blockchain. Files (such as cryptocurrencies or other digital assets) are recorded as belonging to a specific block.

A corresponding "private key" is required to access the associated digital assets. Keeping your private key private is so important that to protect their digital assets from hackers, many people do not keep digital copies of their private keys. They write the number on a piece of paper and keep the paper in a secure location (like a wall safe).

Proof of Work (PoW)

Once a blockchain is instantiated, a Proof of Work algorithm (PoW) is used to create (or "mine") new blocks. The current bitcoin mining technique provides a good example of PoW usage. This technique is described in Wikipedia as follows:

A bitcoin miner runs a computer program that collects unconfirmed transactions from coin dealers in the network. With other data these can form a block and earn a payment to the miner, but a block is accepted by the network only when the miner discovers by trial and error a 'nonce' number that when included in the block yields a hash with a sufficient number of leading zero bits to meet the network's difficulty target. Blocks accepted from miners form the bitcoin blockchain that is a growing ledger of every bitcoin transaction since the coin's first creation.

Proof of Stake (PoS)

There are several other ways for blocks on a blockchain to be validated. One important option is Proof of Stake. We will cover this under Layer 2 Solutions below.

The API (Application Programming Interface)

The next step in the development of a distributed ledger is to set up an API (application programming interface) so that organizations that wish to transact may do so by using the internet. Transaction endpoints allow permission-based access to the data on the blockchain.

The API will also feature a "mining endpoint," which will do three things:

1. Calculate the PoW.

2. Add the transaction and grant the miner a reward (i.e. bitcoins in bitcoin mining).

3. Create a new block and add it to the blockchain.

Peer-to-Peer (Mesh) Networks

Distributed ledgers derive their power from being distributed and decentralized. To accomplish this, a distributed ledger needs a method of accepting new nodes and a way to implement a consensus algorithm to resolve conflicts and to ensure the veracity of the blockchain.

This is done over a P2P or mesh network, a decentralized computer network where each computer (node) acts as both a client (a computer that accesses information on a server) and a server (a computer that serves information to clients). At scale, P2P networks are self-healing and very stable because the information is replicated in thousands (and in some cases millions) of places.

Public or Private

There are two general types of blockchain networks: anonymous networks, where each user has a copy of the entire blockchain and helps process and confirm transactions, and permission-based (non-anonymous) networks, where permission is required to possess a copy of the blockchain and to help process and confirm transactions.

Smart Contracts

A Smart Contract is Like a Vending Machine

Vending machines are a good metaphor for smart contracts. You identify the item you wish to obtain. You put your money in the slot. The vending machine determines if it is the correct amount of money. If it is not the correct amount, the vending machine asks you for more or offers to return the money you have already inserted. If it is the correct amount, the vending machine releases the item you selected.

Smart contracts work exactly the same way. You state your conditions, someone meets the conditions, and the transaction is completed.

Smart Contracts in Action

In practice, smart contracts are self-executing programs that automatically check the rules of the transaction, verify and process the transaction, and (in some cases) enforce the obligations of the parties. As you can imagine, this type of automation has the potential to dramatically increase productivity and lower costs.

Say you want to rent an apartment. You send your landlord your first month's rent plus a security deposit. Since you've met the initial conditions, the smart contract provides a digital entry keycode (via blockchain) by the first of the month.

As long as both parties continue to fulfill their obligations under the agreement (rent is paid, digital entry keycode is available on the blockchain), all is well. If the digital entry keycode does not show up, the smart contract refunds your money. If you don't pay the rent, you don't get a keycode.

Obviously, there would be more conditions to be met and different remedies for grievances. Also (and very importantly) smart contracts do not reduce the need for lawyers, the rule of law, good business practices, good business models, or excellent customer experiences. Smart contracts simply automate transactions without the need for a central authority.

Wait. What?
I Don't Need a Blockchain for That

In the example above, you could easily accomplish the same thing with a well-constructed, secure database and a well-written application with a nice front end.

The Key Question

Why is a blockchain a better solution than a well-structured, secure database?

This may be the most important question you can ask when thinking about using blockchain for any purpose, including blockchain-enabled smart contracts.

How Do I Create Smart Contracts?

Smart contracts can be coded on any blockchain. Ethereum is popular. Regardless of the language you write them in (Solidity, Serpent, LLL, Mutan, etc.), all smart contracts are written (and can be thought of) as if/then statements: "If this happens, then do that."

What Can You Do With Smart Contracts?

The uses for smart contracts are limited only by your imagination. They will reduce costs, human error, paperwork, and manual recordkeeping. They have the potential to increase margins, improve business intelligence, and dramatically increase productivity. If you currently have business processes that would benefit from these improvements, it's time to put away your stone carvings and get digital.

Gas Prices (The Cost of Mining)

"Gas prices" is the term of art for the transaction fees that crypto-miners charge for their services mining ETH on the Ethereum blockchain (a.k.a. its mainnet). "Gas limit" is the maximum amount of ETH you are willing to spend on a particular transaction.

It will not surprise you to learn that miners prioritize the transactions with highest gas prices. Due to the ever-increasing volume of on-chain activity, gas fees have been soaring on Ethereum. However, there is a proposed solution: Layer 2.

Layer 2: The Evolution of Blockchain Technology

You just minted your first NFT. That's hot. You know what's hotter? The Earth. On average, minting a new NFT takes about 130 kWh of electricity. That's about $27 worth of electricity in NYC. Selling your NFT will use about 340 kWh of juice (about $71 per transaction), which is enough electricity to power your whole house for about two weeks or run your refrigerator for a year.

Some environmental watchdogs are saying that a single NFT could, in just a few months, add hundreds of tons of carbon emissions to the atmosphere and meaningfully contribute to global warming.

It's true that blockchains are massive power hogs. When you combine the carbon footprint with the gas prices and the time delay, the whole enterprise seems doomed. Thankfully, this is not a new problem, and the solution has been in the works for years. By the time you read this, we should have several Layer 2 solutions available.

So long miners. Hello minters.

Mining on a mainnet like Ethereum is expensive, time consuming, and highly inefficient. The solu-

Shelly Palmer

tion comes in the form of a new layer sitting on top of the mainnet, cleverly called Layer 2. There are several schemas for Layer 2 solutions, but the general idea is to change the consensus mechanism from Proof of Work (PoW) to Proof of Stake (PoS).

Proof of Stake (PoS)

Proof of Stake is a consensus mechanism for confirming the validity of a block on a blockchain. The benefits include better energy efficiency, lower hardware costs, stronger immunity to centralization, faster transaction times, and low transaction costs. Here's how Ethereum describes PoS:

Proof of stake is the underlying mechanism that activates validators upon receipt of enough stake. For Ethereum, users will need to stake 32 ETH to become a validator. Validators are chosen at random to create blocks and are responsible for checking and confirming blocks they don't create. A user's stake is also used as a way to incentivize good validator behavior. For example, a user can lose a portion of their stake for things like going offline (failing to validate) or their entire stake for deliberate collusion.

Unlike proof of work, validators don't need to use significant amounts of computational power because they're selected at random and aren't competing. They don't need to mine blocks; they just need to create blocks when chosen and validate proposed blocks when they're not. This validation is known as attesting. You can think of attesting as saying "this block looks good to me." Validators get rewards for proposing new blocks and for attesting to ones they've seen. If you attest to malicious blocks, you lose your stake.

Layer 2 solutions are coming online now. Major players include Polygon (formerly Matic), Lightning Network, Counterfactual, Loom Network, and Plasma, among dozens more. At some point in time, maybe by the time you read this, Ethereum will have launched its oft-delayed Layer 2 solution called Optimism.

Decentralization

Decentralization is the most important attribute of platforms built on distributed ledger (blockchain) technology. The ability to conduct business without the need for a central authority is a powerful idea. You can be your own bank. You can set your own contract terms. You are under no obligation to trust anyone. When the conditions of your smart contract are met, a transaction occurs. If the conditions are not met, no value is exchanged.

Some other benefits include:

- Openness: the ability to start trading with just a digital wallet. There's nothing to apply for, and there's no permission required.

- Privacy (or, more accurately, anonymity): you don't need to tell anyone anything about yourself. There are no logins and no email addresses, just your wallet number.

- Transparency: everyone can see every transaction (though not the names of the parties).

DeFi

DeFi (decentralized finance) platforms are the underlying technologies enabling financial services to be offered with no central authority.

Dapps

Dapps (decentralized applications) are apps making the blockchain (distributed ledger ecosystem) run. New Dapps for lending, loans, trading, saving, and even derivative financial instruments are launching every day. *[See Link 2 - shellypalmer. com/blockchain-book-links]* for a list of some organizations, toolsets, and frameworks that offer important component parts to the quickly-evolving DeFi ecosystem.

Cryptocurrencies

Bitcoin

Bitcoin (BTC) is the original cryptocurrency. There are thousands of others.

Altcoins

The term "altcoin" applies to any cryptocurrency other than bitcoin (BTC). Ethereum's Ether (ETH) is the most popular altcoin.

Stablecoins

Cryptocurrencies pegged to fiat currencies are called stablecoins. USDC is pegged to the US Dollar, as is Tether. The upside of a stablecin is reduced volatility, earned interest, and inexpensive swaps and transfers. The downside is that they are pegged to a fiat currency, which means they require trusted third parties, are subject to audits, offer lower ROI, and are regulated.

Crypto Exchanges

Cryptocurrency exchanges act as an intermediary between a buyer and a seller, making money through commissions. You can buy, sell, or trade your crypto for other crypto or fiat currencies. Not all exchanges offer access to all currencies. Choose your exchange carefully to ensure it meets your risk profile, your regulatory requirements, and your trading style. *[See Link 3 - shellypalmer.com/blockchain-book-links]* for a list of the most popular centralized (as well as decentralized) exchanges.

Decentralization is the key feature of cryptocurrency and its underlying technology, so it might surprise you to learn that most cryptocurrency transactions go through centralized exchanges. Centralized exchanges generally offer a higher degree of reliability and, more importantly, a company you can hold accountable for the execution of your transactions. Most (though not all) centralized exchanges must comply with "know your customer" rules and (at least some) regulatory requirements.

Decentralized Cryptocurrency Exchanges (DEX)

Decentralized cryptocurrency exchanges (DEX) allow users to execute transactions without an intermediary, which makes DEX transactions attractive to those who wish to keep their trading activity private. Generally speaking, DEX transactions are crypto-to-crypto; decentralized exchanges do not facilitate transactions between crypto and fiat currencies.

Centralized DeFi: an oxymoron

Some of the biggest and most popular names in crypto are not actually decentralized. Coinbase, for example, is an extremely popular and reputable crypto exchange that went public in mid-2021. It is also a central authority. There is absolutely nothing about Coinbase that is decentralized, and you cannot include it (or any other centralized exchange) in the DeFi universe.

Digital Wallets

You will need at least one crypto wallet. Do your research as each wallet has its pros and cons, and no single wallet is right for everyone or for every application. There are dozens (if not hundreds) of crypto wallets available. *[See Link 4 - shellypalmer.com/blockchain-book-links]* for a short list of well-established digital wallets.

Encrypting Your Crypto

The moment comes when you realize there's real money in your crypto wallet and you start wondering about hackers and ransomware and all kinds of bad stuff. If you've set up a digital wallet, bought some crypto, and collected a few NFTs and you're starting to trade across a range of marketplaces and exchanges, you are starting to experience the exceptional financial freedom the world of DeFi has to offer. Of course, there's a catch... Now, you're also in charge of guarding the treasury.

This is exactly as scary as it sounds, which is one of the main reasons people put their money in banks. Not only are banks good at protecting your money, in the United States, you can choose bank accounts that are insured by the Federal Deposit Insurance Corporation or the National Credit Union Administration so if something happens to the bank, your money is still safe.

In lieu of safety, or insurance, or even customer service, DeFi transactions come with a warning: "All transactions final." And an admonition: "Protect yourself at all times."

Guarding the Vault

It is in the spirit of this last little bit of wisdom that I offer some workflow and process to help you protect your crypto holdings.

First, make sure you are using a name brand digital wallet. There are software wallets and hardware wallets. You should have both. When choosing a wallet, make sure that it is compatible with the cryptocurrency you want to store in it.

Use your hardware wallets to store the crypto you are hodling (crypto-slang for holding). That's wallets. Plural. If you have a substantial sum of crypto, you should keep it in several different wallets. My suggestion is to have the percentage of tokens in any given wallet allocated to mirror your portfolio. A mix of coins. It probably goes without saying, but don't put all your crypto in one wallet. Ever!

There are several popular hardware wallets. I am a fan of the Ledger Nano X and the Trezor Model T. I don't have a relationship with either company; I purchase my wallets retail directly from their respective sites. There are some promo codes to be found online, but for reasons that will become obvious as you read on, only purchase your hardware wallets directly from the manufacturer's website. Do not break this rule. Purchase enough wallets (from more than one vendor) to split your portfolio up into thirds or more. Don't put all your crypto in one wallet. Ever! (Did I mention that before?)

You can keep a small amount of crypto in software wallets. There are many to choose from. Because of its browser extension, Metamask is a great utility wallet. There's also Coinomi, Coinbase Wallet, Trust Wallet, Exodus, Electrum, Mycelium ... the list is long. Some have fully functional smartphone apps, and others have apps that give you visibility into your wallet but don't offer access. Some apps are Bluetooth; others use the web. No matter which one you choose, just keep enough crypto in your software wallets to do your daily crypto business. Whatever you're hodling, keep it offline!

Storing Your Passwords and Recovery Phrases

No matter which wallets you choose, you will set them up with a password or pin and they will almost certainly require a 12- or 24-word recovery phrase. If you've never set up a digital wallet, go to Metamask *[See Link 5 - shellypalmer.com/blockchain-book-links]* and set one up. You don't need to put any crypto into it. You never need to use it, but you should go through the process of setting up a secure digital wallet. When you're done, you will have two important things to write down: your password or pin, and your recovery phrase. Where will you store them for safekeeping?

A Trusted Family Member or Friend

You need to make sure that someone (other than you) has access to the records and understands exactly where your physical hardware wallets are hidden, and where the computer or smartphone with your software wallets is located. Otherwise, if something happens to you, your crypto goes with you.

Old School

You can write down your password and recovery phrase on a piece of paper and store the paper in a safe or safety deposit box or wherever you keep important documents. But understand that you will change your passwords quite often and you are going to have several wallets. Paper records are fine. I would suggest doing this no matter what other solutions you choose.

Slightly Newer School

For a mostly safe way to store your wallet information on your computer, you can copy and paste it into a Microsoft Word or Excel document and encrypt the file when you save it. File>Info>Protect Workbook (Document), then enter your document password, then confirm it, and your document cannot be opened without that password. It's pretty good protection, and if you don't name the document something like "My Crypto Passwords," it won't be found by a casual snooper.

Your Inner James Bond

To take it up a notch, take a new USB drive (flash drive, thumb drive, USB stick) and when you open it, right click it and select "Turn on Bitlocker" on a Windows PC, or "Encrypt" on a Mac. Linux peeps, *[See Link 6 - shellypalmer.com/blockchain-*

Shelly Palmer

book-links] for a set of instructions. Once you've encrypted and password protected the USB drive, save your encrypted, password-protected documents to it and remove them from your computer. You don't need to put the USB drive in a safe (unless you want to); you can just keep it in a safe place. The info on it is about as safe as it can be in a digital world. This solution will only work on one operating system. So Mac encryption is readable on a Mac, Windows on a Windows PC, etc. Some cross-platform commercial encryption software is available, but I have not had wonderful experiences with any of it. Bitlocker works. Encrypt works. The Linux encryption sequence I linked to above works.

Channeling Tony Stark

There's always a next level. You can purchase a hardware-encrypted USB drive. They are expensive. On the other hand, if you feel you need even more protection, Kingston's IronKey or Apricorn Aegis Secure Key or other so-called military-grade encrypted USB drives may work for you. Some of these drives (the expensive ones) have self-destruct capabilities if too many failed login attempts happen in a row. Others offer higher levels of security or speed. Because they are hardware based, almost all of these drives will work on any computer platform.

Where You Are Most Vulnerable

Do not get too crazy with encryption. It is not your first line of defense. Use strong passwords on your computer and make sure your antivirus software is up to date. If you truly want to protect your "vault," keep it offline as much as possible. This can be accomplished by dedicating a PC or Mac as "crypto only." By dedicating, I mean nothing is on the computer but your wallet software and a browser – not Zoom, not Netflix, not email – nothing but your crypto software.

The reason for this is simple. You are the weakest link in your online security. The doing of online business happens on your computer and your smartphone. You can do online banking with a bank because they are doing all the security for you. When you are both banker and security team, you need to reduce, to the highest extent possible, common attack vectors. Isolated, dedicated hardware and software reduce your likelihood of clicking on something you shouldn't click on.

Non-Fungible Tokens (NFTs)

The most famous type of smart contracts are NFTs. In principle, an NFT is exactly the opposite of a cryptocurrency. By definition, all cryptocurriences are fungible. Said differently, your bitcoin

Shelly Palmer

and my bitcoin are worth exactly the same amount of fiat currency, which means that we can easily trade one for another. NFTs are non-fungible. In principle, each NFT is unique, so you cannot trade one for another as each has a market value of its own. In the physical world, most of the things we own are non-fungible. Your car and my car are both cars, but they cannot be exchanged for one another. This is also true of houses, most clothing, and most jewelry.

The two most widely-used NFT standards are smart contracts written and stored on the Ethereum blockchain:

- **ERC-721:** A standard interface for non-fungible tokens, also known as deeds.

- **ERC-1155:** A standard interface for contracts that manage multiple token types. A single deployed contract may include any combination of fungible tokens, non-fungible tokens, or other configurations (e.g. semi-fungible tokens).

NFTs are created ("minted") when a unique, standardized token and associated smart contract are recorded on a blockchain. In theory, NFTs are non-fungible. Said differently, the NFT of Nyan Cat (which sold at auction for roughly $560,000) is unique and not interchangeable with other versions of the same file. *[See Link 7 - shellypalmer. com/blockchain-book-links]* for a list of popular sites where you can mint your own NFTs.

Using NFTs for Fan or Audience Development

People have started using the term "NFT" interchangeably with the term "digital collectible." This is unfortunate, because while most of the digital collectibles in the news are NFTs, the technology can be used to create value in many additional ways. When thinking about fan or audience development, which we will define as a collection of purpose-built tools designed to grow communities of interest, perhaps the most obvious use for an NFT is as a ticket to an event. Let's review some of the benefits you might expect from combining a ticket, some unique digital assets, and a smart contract.

NFTs are Smart Contracts

All NFTs are smart contracts. A smart contract is just like an old-fashioned verbal or paper contract, except with a smart contract, when the conditions are met (digitally), the contract executes automatically. Immutable, self-executing contracts coupled with the automatic exchange of funds (or tokens) open up a world of possibilities for ticketing.

The Elimination of Duplicate or Fraud-ulent Tickets

Every NFT is unique, and ownership is written on a public distributed ledger (blockchain) which can be read by anyone. If your ownership of an NFT has been validated, a quick matching of public and private keys (using something as common as a bar-code reader) would instantly verify that the person with the NFT in their digital wallet was the authentic owner of the ticket.

Revenue from Secondary Markets

If someone sells their NFT ticket, that transaction can trigger royalty payments to the issuer as well as any other stakeholder – artists, sports leagues, athletes, sponsors, promoters, a charity, or literally anyone with a digital wallet. These business rules can be hard-coded into each NFT, and like all smart contracts, when a transaction occurs and the conditions are met, funds automatically change hands.

Visibility into Transactions

Bots, scalpers, bad actors, criminals, and 2nd-party sales on eBay or other auction sites are common. NFT tickets offer an easy way to gather actionable business intelligence about how and where your tickets are being sold and resold. You can find the exact moment of the transaction, the exact address of the digital wallets in use, the amount of the transaction, and much, much more. Contrary to popular mythology, NFT transactions are not anonymous. There are several commercial firms such as Chainalysis and CipherTrace that offer blockchain BI tools.

Reduced Ticketing Costs

NFTs are not mined, they are minted. This is a non-trivial technical distinction. Today, you can mint NFT tickets for less than 10 cents apiece — and the price of NFT ticket production will continue to drop.

New Revenue

You can, of course, mint NFT tickets as stand-alone digital collectibles. But you can also use NFT tickets to allow fans access to an auction where they might bid on NFTs containing more valuable exclusive content. Because of the NFTs ability to collect 1st party data, they can also be used to augment loyalty programs. The marketing techniques will need to be tested, but the technological capability is built in.

Data-driven Marketing Opportunities

Today, if you purchase six tickets to a sporting event and bring five family members or friends, the ticket seller has a business relationship with you but has no information about the other five people in your party. NFTs have the power to change that. If each attendee was required to present an NFT for entrance, the NFT would need to be transferred to their personal digital wallets. Depending upon how you wrote the business logic and what data you asked for as a condition of the ticket sale, the NFTs could collect a wealth of actionable first-party data.

DeFi Opportunities

NFTs can be bought, sold, traded, swapped, used as collateral, borrowed, lent, etc. In other words, your ability to financially engineer to create additional value is only limited by your creativity and your audience's willingness to participate. The blockchain's ability to democratize finance is part of what makes the technology super-exciting, super-dangerous, super-volatile and awesome! It is also why the world of crypto and DeFi (decentralized finance), writ large, has the attention of governments and regulators worldwide.

Next-level Marketing

Whether your audience is a community of interest, a community of practice, or a community of passion, next-level marketers will have the opportunity to let their imaginations run free. What does your audience value the most? How can you empower them to participate? What additional value can you help them obtain? What is the next generation of loyalty program? How much "access" to the star attraction can they achieve? Smart contracts will give smart marketers the tools they need to design new kinds of marketing programs with ongoing, automated value-creation components built in.

What's Next

Traditional ticketing software has been a race to the bottom. Most of the systems are old and tired. Not surprisingly, almost every major ticketing company has announced that they are planning or already working on or about to launch a new NFT ticketing product. This is great. While there will be way too many different approaches, some will emerge as better than others. Consumers will vote with their wallets (as they always do), and this new tech will evolve.

Importantly, some of the most interesting blockchain projects are polychains or multichains which

Shelly Palmer

are being built to aggregate disparate blockchains. These new blockchains of blockchains will empower Web 3.0 and certainly play some role in the evolution of NFT ticketing. In the meantime, I hope some of these ideas resonate with you and get you thinking about new ways to create value for your business.

When Will Crypto Be Useful?

Enrobed in a purple satin vestment as interesting, eccentric, and colorful as the man himself, Mike Novogratz, the high priest of Crypto, thrilled and delighted his disciples, adherents, and devotees from the main stage of Bitcoin2021 Miami. Confirming what the audience of crypto-revelers already deeply believe, the crypto-billionaire explained, "What gives it [value] is this social construct, that we believe it's got value. It's the narrative. And so we need more and more storytellers, and the optimism is, we're gettin' 'em. (Applause)." Mr. Novogratz has a good reason to believe that crypto is valuable. In March 2021, he revealed that cryptocurrencies made up nearly 85% ($4.8 billion) of his $5.65 billion net worth.

Awareness is not the issue

Practically everyone has heard of crypto. But as fun and interesting as investing in a new asset class on new trading platforms may be, the market cap of all the crypto ever created represents under $2 trillion, which is about 0.2% of the estimated $1 quadrillion of accumulated wealth in the world. Said differently, to grow to any significant size, cryptocurrency is going to have to become as useful and accessible as fiat currency. This isn't an awareness issue, and it isn't an issue you can solve with storytelling. It's a technical issue – a big one, actually.

Secure. Decentralized. Pick any two.

The promise of Decentralized Finance (DeFi) is the financial freedom afforded by three critical attributes: scale, security, and decentralization. Unfortunately, there are some significant technical hurdles preventing any system from attaining full measures of all three. So, in practice, your network can be big and secure, or decentralized and secure, or big and decentralized. But it cannot be big, decentralized, and secure.

Visa

According to Visa, there are approximately 3.3 billion Visa cards worldwide and VisaNet, the company's global processing network, can handle more than 65,000 tps (transactions per second). On an average day, Visa only processes about 2,000 tps, but it's nice to know that if everyone on earth had a Visa card, VisaNet wouldn't blink. Fast, secure, reliable payments are core values for Visa. It has been scaled to global proportions, and it is one of the most secure financial networks in the world. But, alas, it is centralized.

Bitcoin

By comparison, a Bitcoin block holding between 2,500 and 2,700 transactions gets mined about every 10 minutes. This translates to ~5 tps. So, in practice, you can't have 3.3 billion people spending Bitcoin. It would be impossible to confirm the transactions in any reasonable timeframe.

How about mining bigger blocks?

Bitcoin blocks are 1 MB each. As of May 16, 2021, the Bitcoin blockchain was ~337.35 GB. Remember, the entire Bitcoin blockchain must reside on all ~11,000 nodes in the Bitcoin network. *[See Link 8 - shellypalmer.com/blockchain-book-links]* to learn how to run your own full node. This means each new 1 MB block must be transmitted through a peer-to-peer network over the public internet to ~11,000 computers. This takes about 14 seconds.

You can make the blocks bigger, but bigger blocks mean a bigger blockchain. At a certain point, only massive data centers would be able to hold full copies, which would "centralize" the world's first decentralized cryptocurrency.

It should be noted that Bitcoin's slow transaction speed is traded off for exceptional decentralization and security. Ethereum is in the same boat.

Layer 2 to the rescue!

The promise of Layer 2 solutions (such as Ethereum's Optimism) is that they will scale because they are much, much faster. But imagine the following: you build a Layer 2 solution that can handle 1,000 tps. That's excellent scale. You grow your community to 2,000 nodes. That's excellent decentralization. Your Proof of Stake protocol calls for 1,001 validators to confirm each block. That's excellent security. Problem solved! Except it isn't solved, because now lots of people are starting to use your network to do ordinary things and the peer-to-peer networks over the public internet can't handle the amount of data you need to move around to keep all your validation nodes in sync. So you have two choices. You can reduce the number of validators (reducing security) or you can put the validators in commercial data centers where the internet speeds are not an issue (reducing decentralization). Like I said: scale, security, and decentralization. Pick any two.

The Workaround

This is one of those "deep in the weeds" problems most people ignore because they are sure that some smart engineers will work it out. And even if that's not possible, they figure the exponential rate of technological change we experience in the normal course of our lives is sure to provide a solution. Maybe. In the meantime, Polygon and Polkadot are doing exceptional work in this area. I am a huge fan of both. And even with the trade offs we're exploring here, Layer 2 solutions are going to change the world.

That said, you're going to have to pay close attention to the strategies and philosophies of this new class of DeFi solutions. Each new network and protocol — in fact, every blockchain-based solution, will have to be designed to balance security, scalability, and decentralization for its specific use case. You will want to be well aware of those tradeoffs.

The downside to these workarounds is that we are likely to see an explosion of centralized high-performance blockchains that people will not recognize as such. Governments will use them for central bank digital currency (CBDC), vaccine passports, tax records, PHI, PII, and, sadly, a bunch of other surveillance-state, Orwellian stuff that nightmares are made of.

You will make crypto useful

Mike Novogratz has it right. You are the most important part of the DeFi story. Like all tech, DeFi is evolving at an exponential rate. So just pretend everything you can imagine is already possible. Take a moment to "blue sky" a new business model that would thrive in a world where value could be exchanged as easily as information. When you invent and build a business that profits or grows by leveraging DeFi or you start exchanging cryptocurrency for everyday goods and services, crypto will evolve into an asset class that is both valuable *and* useful.

Web 3.0
Things You Should Know

The next generation of the World Wide Web (Web 3.0) is being built on blockchains using tools and technologies similar to the ones that empower cryptocurrency, NFTs, smart contracts, and the world of DeFi. If Web 3.0 reaches its full potential, it will quite literally change the world. That's a bold claim, so we need some bold evidence. Let's start with a little demonstration.

If you click *[See Link 9 - shellypalmer.com/block-chain-book-links]*, you will be taken to a page that looks very much like this one. Except the page is not being served from a web server; you'll be reading a single web page I uploaded to a decentralized database called IPFS (the InterPlanetary File System). This blockchain-powered, peer-to-peer database offers many of the features and benefits we may come to expect from Web 3.0 applications, so it's a great place to see the ancestral DNA of Web 3.0 start to take form. *[See Link 10 - shellypalmer. com/blockchain-book-links]* to see a "pinned" link to the same file. Explanation below.)

A Super-brief History of the Interweb

The internet predates the World Wide Web by almost 30 years. Web 1.0 (which we will define as static HTML pages viewable in a browser over a TCP/IP connection) shows up in the mid-90s. About a decade later, the advent of Web 2.0 brings dynamic websites and applications as well as audio and video streaming. It's the web as you know it today. The goal of Web 3.0 is to decentralize the World Wide Web and put you in charge of your data. In this case, "to decentralize" specifically means ending the dominance of big tech.

Web 2.0 Location. Location. Location.

To access content using a Web 2.0 browser, you enter a URL (Uniform Resource Locator). Said differently, you need to know the "location" of the resource you wish to access. For example, www. shellypalmer.com is located at 199.16.172.35. A DNS (domain name server) keeps an index of which name matches which location (address).

Web 3.0 "May I See Your Content ID Please?"

Web 3.0 websites and apps can't have a location; the content is distributed over peer-to-peer networks, so instead of using a URL, you find your distributed content with a unique content identifier or CID. (This is IPFS nomenclature and may not be a term used by other applications, but it is conceptually correct.)

Web 3.0 Content Is Immutable

This is where Web 3.0 starts to get interesting, because you are distributing unique content to a peer-to-peer network. Once the content becomes available on the network, it is immutable. You can't edit, replace, or delete it. Each update generates a new CID. (We'll get to how you update files stored on IPFS in a minute.) Let this sink in. Every page is forever. For reference, most Web 2.0 webpages last about 100 days online.

The following are IPFS specific, so to avoid confusion, the next few paragraphs describe features of IPFS and not necessarily features of all (or any oth-

er) Web 3.0 applications. While the terminology may be different, any decentralized storage solution will share some (or all) of these ideas.

DHTs Replace DNS (Alphabet Soup)

Time for some overly geeky stuff. Instead of a DNS, IPFS content is mapped using Distributed Hash Tables (DHTs). Repeat after me: "The DHT maps the CID and the peer IP address." Every peer (client/server) node that wants to share your content will have a copy of a DHT that identifies your content.

So What Makes IPFS Publishing Different?

When you publish a file you want to share on IPFS, a new CID is generated. Your local DHT is updated and, until someone else downloads your content, you are the only computer serving your content. All the DHTs of your content peers will automatically be updated, but they will only have your specific IP address until others begin to download your files. This small window (before anyone downloads your content) is the only time you can actually delete a file (because it's the last time it will only be on your computer). Once the content is out in the world, it will be there forever.

Updating Immutable Files

The concept of immutable content is very "block-chainy." Technically, whatever you write to a block-chain is immutable and forever. But as interesting as immutable content may be for some applications, websites are dynamic, data is dynamic, prices are dynamic, typos need to get fixed, graphics need updating, etc. The IPFS workaround is simple. Instead of sharing the CID of your content, you hash your public key and share it. In an IPFS application, a hashed public key will do the job that a URL does for a Web 2.0 website. There are also third-party "pinning" services such as Pinata that address this issue.

This Is Just the Beginning

There is much more to this story. I used IPFS to help me tell a small part of the story of Web 3.0, but there are many other Dapps (decentralized applications) that you should explore to get a better understanding of the art of the possible. To start, have a look at other decentralized storage solutions such as Storj or the venerable, but very up-to-date, BitTorrent.

More Great Use Cases for Blockchain

Blockchain is well-known for being Bitcoin's underlying technology, but many believe blockchain has the power to radically transform entire industries. You already know about smart contracts, so below are five more non-cryptocurrency blockchain (distributed ledger) use cases to help you form your own opinion.

Tokenization of Content

Overview: Tokenization allows you to take an asset and fractionalize its ownership by creating digital tokens. Each token represents a percentage of ownership in the asset, and the use of blockchain makes the chain of custody and proof of ownership immutable. In practice, you can do this with both digital and physical assets, but in the absence of laws or regulations, claiming title to physical property without proper government records tends to yield unexpected results. That said, there are quite a few tokenization projects in the works.

Use Cases: Tokenizing content allowed messaging app Kik to have a "reverse ICO (initial coin offering)" in which the company decentralized itself by selling tokens, like stocks, to interested investors to raise $100 million and continue to grow its platform. Simple Token empowers companies to easily create branded tokens without having to worry about regulatory issues or creating an ICO.

Eliminating Counterfeit Products

Overview: Because blockchains are permanent, immutable ledgers, it's easy to identify and trace the chain of ownership of assets. Storing serial numbers (or other product identity information on a blockchain) allows all parties (manufacturers, distributors, retailers, and consumers) to verify that the item in question is authentic.

Use Cases: Blockverify uses blockchain technology to boost anti-counterfeit measures by helping to identify counterfeits and prevent counterfeit duplication of products and by enabling companies to verify their products and monitor their supply chains. The world's largest diamond producer, De Beers, is working with blockchain technology to create an immutable and permanent digital record for every registered diamond in order to cut down on conflict ("blood") diamonds.

Supply Chain Improvement

Overview: By identifying production components and processes and by storing that information on a blockchain, you can monitor (and optimize) your supply chain from raw materials to finished goods.

Use Cases: Walmart uses blockchain to allow its employees to scan goods (like fruit) in the store's app and track it along every step of the journey from harvest to store floor. The world's largest shipping company, Maersk, uses blockchain to monitor its cargo ships. British Airways uses blockchain to ensure the information it shares on its site, in its apps, and on airport displays is up-to-date and correct.

Digital Twins

Overview: A digital twin is a virtual representation of a physical asset. Through sensor data, artificial intelligence, and human input, digital twins mirror their real world counterparts and create value by allowing for training, maintenance, troubleshooting, simulation, and more.

Use Cases: Deloitte uses digital twins to "detect physical issues sooner, predict outcomes more accurately, and build better products," while GE uses digital twins to optimize its wind farms, which led to an increase of up to 20% in annual energy production.

Encrypted Messaging

Overview: Encrypted messaging has become table stakes for business communication. There are many traditional solutions for end-to-end encryption, but blockchain has inspired an approach that leverages decentralization. Using blockchain, messages can be anonymous (even IP addresses can be masked). Work is generally done locally, so no private user data is transferred, and some blockchain-based encrypted messaging solutions include anonymous cryptocurrency-style payment options as well.

Use Cases: There are quite a few organizations working on blockchain-powered encrypted messaging platforms, including Matrix, Crypviser, and ADAMANT.

How Crypto-Mining Works

One of the best ways to learn about cryptocurrency is to mine some for yourself. In the spirit of pure education, here's how to build a very small cryptocurrency mining operation of your very own.

Crypto and NFTs (Two Sides of a Coin)

Cryptocurrencies, such as ETH or BTC, are created ("mined") when a miner completes a certain amount of computations used to verify transactions added to a specific blockchain. The miner is rewarded for this effort with a small amount of cryptocurrency. In theory, every ETH or BTC is fungible. Said differently, my 10 BTC or my 50 ETH are worth exactly what your 10 BTC or 50 ETH are worth, and they are interchangeable.

Unique, immutable records of cryptocoins and NFTs are stored on blockchains that rely on vast networks of individual mining operations and mining pools. You're about to jump into a mining pool, but the water is far from fine. Please read the following disclaimer very, very carefully.

Disclaimer: If you've read this far, you are a serious newbie. That's awesome. This is the kind of science project you used to love as a kid. However, we are about to jump into a super-complicated, extremely dangerous world where charlatans, hucksters, and flat-out criminals are indistinguishable from others. If you choose to follow the steps outlined below, please use a spare computer that you don't need for anything else. It should not have any data on it at all – none! Just the operating system and files you absolutely do not care about. You do NOT want to do this on a computer that you use for business. You do NOT want to do this on a computer that has any personal information on it. I cannot say this strongly enough. This is an educational exercise, and the first lesson is, "Protect yourself at all times."

Equipment Requirements

For this exercise, you will need a Windows computer with a decent video (graphics) card. Since this is just a science project, any Windows computer will do. For this example I used a mid-level gaming computer running Windows 10 Home. (For geeks, it has an i7 9700 (10th Gen), 48 GB RAM, an NVIDIA 2080 Ti 11GB video card, and an 850W power supply.)

Importantly, this example is 100% about the GPU (graphics processing unit), a.k.a. the video card. The processor does almost no work, and very little RAM on the motherboard is used. This example is the reason that fully-loaded cargo planes filled with NVIDIA graphics cards leave for Asia every day. (High-end GPUs are also great for AI and eSports. To say they are in short supply is to seriously understate the issue.)

Step 1: Your Crypto Wallet

It doesn't make sense to mine crypto if you don't have a place to put it. You will need a crypto wallet. There are dozens of them. I am partial to hardware wallets, but for this exercise, we are going to use Coinomi, which you will find at coinomi.com.

The benefits of Coinomi is that it is simple to install, simple to set up, and compatible with a large number of different cryptocurrencies. Even if you have other wallets set up, create a new wallet in Coinomi for this exercise. Download the software and carefully follow the instructions.

Shelly Palmer

Step 2: Join a Mining Pool

To keep this simple, we're going to mine Ether (ETH). To do this, we're going to join a very popular mining pool called Ethermine.

When it's time to configure your Windows .bat files to start mining, you will choose the servers closest to you. Power is key to all of this, so choose a server close to you.

Step 3: Connect your Coinomi Wallet to Ethermine

Pro tip: You will probably need to know the public IP address of your mining computer. *[See Link 11 - shellypalmer.com/blockchain-book-links]*.

Step 4: Download and Configure Your Mining Software

If you scroll down this page *[See Link 12 - shellypalmer.com/blockchain-book-links]*, you'll see Phoenix Miner Download & Configuration Guide. Go for it. You must configure the mining software to work with the Ethermine pool. Follow the instructions carefully and to the letter. Once this is done, you can start mining. (Yes, it's that simple.) But... you're not really done yet. Important note: there is a version of Phoenix Miner on the public internet that is suspected to be malware. The only link you should trust is the link found on the ethermine.org start page. Do NOT download Phoenix Miner from any other link.

Step 5: Overclock and Tune Your GPU

The story of mining is efficiency. Power costs money. Wasted power damages the environment. Profitable mining is a delicate balance between speed, power, and accuracy. If your computer has a separate GPU, download MSI Afterburner *[See Link 2 - shellypalmer.com/blockchain-book-links]* and fire it up. Please note that overclocking your GPU (or your CPU for that matter) can literally destroy your computer, so don't go crazy. Limit your GPU power to a maximum of 70%, which is pretty safe. You can leave your GPU fan on auto, but if you want to be really safe, turn off the auto function, crank the fan to 80%, and leave it there. It will be loud, but your GPU will be safe. Don't touch the core clock or the memory clock settings until you read more about this. My goal here is to keep your GPU safe; you can mess it up all you like later.

Step 6: Start mining!

Open a browser window with your mining pool, run Afterburner so you can see what's going on with your GPU, and start Phoenix to begin mining ETH.

Shelly Palmer

Are you making money?

Using the system I've described here (with some rudimentary overclocking and GPU tuning), my GPU is drawing just over 175 watts to compute at a hash rate of roughly 53.5 MH/s (mega hashes per second), but my rig is only averaging 51.4 MH/s in the pool. At this hash rate, I've been averaging about 0.00248 ETH per day. Is that profitable? To get a good idea of just how unprofitable a single GPU rig is (remember, you need to amortize the cost of your computer as part of your profit calculations), visit whattomine.com and enter in the model number of your GPU, your cost of electricity, and average hash rate.

Last time I did the full calculation (Christmas Eve 2020), it required a rig capable of roughly 16,000 MH/s to mine one ETH per day. To get to that speed, you'd need dozens (if not hundreds) of better GPUs than the one I used. Setting up a mining operation for fun is easy. Building a business using efficient tools is something else entirely. There are thousands of commercial crypto mining operations around the globe. It is a world you should become very familiar with.

What Is Encryption?

Encryption is the process of using algorithms to

encode information with the specific goal of preventing unauthorized parties from accessing it. For digital communication, there are two popular methods of encryption: symmetric key and public key.

- **Symmetric key encryption** requires both the sending and receiving parties to have the same key, hence the term "symmetric."

- **Public key encryption** is far more popular because the encryption key is publicly available, but only the receiving party has access to the decryption key.

How Can There Be Such a Thing as a "Public" Encryption Key?

One of the most popular ways to create public encryption keys is to use a mathematical problem known as prime factorization (a.k.a. integer factorization). Start with two relatively large prime numbers. (Quick sixth grade math Refresher: a prime number is only divisible by 1 and itself.) Let's call them P1 and P2. When you multiply them, the product is a composite number we'll call "C."

$(P_1 \times P_2 = C)$

C is a very special number with very special properties. It's called a semiprime number, which is only divisible by 1, itself, and the two prime factors that made it. This special property enables the number to be used for public key encryption.

You use C for the public key, and you keep P1 and P2 as the private key pair. While it is very easy to generate C, if the number is large enough and thoughtfully generated, it can take thousands, millions, billions, or even trillions of tries to factor. (There are mathematical strategies to speed up the process, but in practice, prime factoring must be done by trial and error.)

Pretty Good Privacy: The Encryption We Mostly Use

The OpenPGP standard is one of the most popular versions of public key encryption, a.k.a. Pretty Good Privacy or PGP. There is a very good chance that your corporate IT department uses some version of PGP to encrypt your files. After all, it's pretty good.

How good? Using current computer technology, a 2048-bit OpenPGP encrypted file cannot be decrypted. Someday, it might be possible with a fully functional quantum computer, but these are still (for all practical purposes) theoretical devices.

Now, you may push back with an argument like, "Shelly, you may think that a file encoded with

2048-bit OpenPGP encryption is unbreakable, but you don't know that for sure. You have no idea what the NSA can or cannot do! How do you know that quantum computers don't exist? Nothing is impossible!"

Yeah... no. 2048-bit OpenPGP encryption can't be decrypted without a key because of the way computers work today. In the future, with new hardware, processor, and bus speeds that are currently undreamt of, the computation may be able to be done in reasonable time. Not today. Without your private key, the computational time required to break a 2048-bit key in a secure SSL certificate would take more than 6.4 quadrillion years. *[See Link 13 - shellypalmer.com/blockchain-book-links]*

Encryption enables banking (commercial and consumer) and commerce. Without it, the privacy we enjoy in our digital lives would be not be possible.

ICOs: What You Need to Know

Floyd "Money" Mayweather made headlines in 2017 for making light work of Mixed Martial Arts superstar Conor McGregor. He also made tech headlines by endorsing the Hubii Network, an initial coin offering (ICO), on his Instagram and Twitter accounts.

This isn't the first time Mayweather, who has since dubbed himself Floyd "Crypto" Mayweather, has endorsed an ICO. In July 2017, he promoted the ICO for the Stox project, which went on to raise more than $30 million in its token sale. (Note: There are subtle differences between an ICO, a token sale, and a crowdsale. Search the terms to learn more.)

What Is an ICO?

An ICO is similar to an IPO (initial public offering) in that it offers a certain amount of ownership in a company to the public. In an IPO, a share of stock represents fractional ownership of a corporation. In an ICO, a crypto coin represents a percentage of ownership in pretty much any business endeavor (as described in the ICO's documentation).

In an IPO, new shareholders hope that the value of their shares will increase over time. In an ICO, investors are hoping that the value of the newly minted crypto coin will increase. The major difference is that, as of this writing, there are few government rules or regulations that apply to an ICO. Regulators are working hard to get control of the ICO and cryptocurrency markets, and it won't be the Wild Wild West for long. If you want to stage an ICO for your-name-goes-here-coin, now is the time to go for it!

An ICO is about as easy to do as a Kickstarter project. As such, it can make unverified claims about how great the product is or how smart you would be if you invested in it. There's nothing stopping the person or team behind the ICO from taking your money and running for the hills. The Cointelegraph reports that phishing, Ponzi schemes, and other scams account for about 10% of ICOs.

How Does an ICO Work?

When you buy "coins" in an ICO, you're essentially buying digital coupons issued on a blockchain, which you can then trade or hold. While blockchain is a key component to any ICO, Smith + Crown notes that some ICOs are launching "meta-tokens" built on established cryptocurrencies, like Bitcoin.

There Absolutely Is a Criminal Element – But...

Anyone who remembers the problems of Mt. Gox knows cryptocurrency is far from a brand-safe, risk-free industry. Smith + Crown notes that many ICOs are marketed as "software presale tokens" (much like an early access video game on a gaming platform like Steam), using words like "crowdsale" or "donation" (rather than ICO) to avoid legal requirements. This lack of regulation and oversight allows for quick growth, pivots, and innovation, but also leaves less educated investors in the hands of potential bad guys.

Should you be considering your own ICO? "Palmercoin" has a nice ring to it. But, for reasons that should be obvious, I haven't pulled the trigger.

The Philosophical Side of DeFi

Is Cryptocurrency: Money, Currency or Something Else?

Here are 10 reasons why a US dollar is worth the paper it's printed on:

- USS Nimitz (CVN-68)

- USS Dwight D. Eisenhower (CVN-69)

- USS Carl Vinson (CVN-70)

- USS Theodore Roosevelt (CVN-71)

- USS Abraham Lincoln (CVN-72)

- USS George Washington (CVN-73)

- USS John C. Stennis (CVN-74)

- USS Harry S. Truman (CVN-75)

- USS Ronald Reagan (CVN-76)

- USS George H.W. Bush (CVN-77)

There are 18 additional reasons, 14 of which are Ohio-class Trident II SSBN (ship, submersible, ballistic, nuclear) submarines capable of carrying 24 SLBMs (submarine-launched ballistic missiles) on active duty on any given day. The other four are converted Trident 1 subs that each carry 154 Tomahawk missiles.

A reserve currency (or anchor currency) is a currency held in significant quantities by governments and institutions as part of their foreign exchange reserves and is commonly used in international transactions. The U.S. dollar is the world's reserve currency.

There are many component parts that combine to give a U.S. dollar value. Trust, our legal system, and property rights (both real and intellectual) are hugely important, and (of course) that list of military hardware helps quite a bit, too.

What Cryptocurrency is All About

At first glance, cryptocurrency is different from a fiat currency such as a U.S. Dollar. People argue that crypto is virtual currency with no government, land, or physical goods to back it up, making it somehow less valuable than fiat currencies.

While I agree that crypto is different from fiat currency, I disagree with the argument that crypto is, by default, less valuable than fiat currency. Cryptocurrencies are a commodity like gold, copper, or coal. In the case of bitcoin, just like a natural resource, there is a finite quantity. In the case of gold, copper, or coal, there are estimates in the millions, billions, or even trillions of tons. For bitcoin, there will only ever be approximately 21 million, which will become harder and harder to mine. According to the bitcoin FAQ, "The last block that will generate coins will be block #6,929,999, which should be generated at or near the year 2140. The total number of coins in circulation will then remain static at 20,999,999.9769 BTC." Bitcoins are not virtual; they are a commodity that is commonly traded.

When speaking with financial professionals and economists, I am told that all monetary systems are, at their core, belief systems. Gold has some physical attributes that made it an easy choice for a pre-digital civilization to use as a store of value, but it is far from the rarest metal on earth. In practice, gold is probably easier to mine than most cryptocurrencies. Scarcity is not what makes people believe in gold. What will make people believe in crypto?

Tales from under the Merkle Tree

As she approached the entrance to the club, she gave the frame of her new prescription AR glasses a gentle squeeze. When she got to the door, it appeared to turn green, indicating recognition that she was over 21 years of age. A message appeared along with a friendly voice asking for the 5 ADA cover charge. She nodded her head yes. A moment later, the door opened, indicating that the transaction had cleared. So begins a story about life in a trustless, decentralized world... a tale from under the Merkle tree.

Crypto

Ralph C. Merkle is one of the inventors of public-key cryptography, the cryptographic system that enables secure online transactions for banking, ecommerce, and the like. As world-changing as that invention was, his work on the cryptographic hash function and the security and efficiency of his eponymous Merkle tree are even more impressive. If you haven't guessed by now, the "crypto" in cryptocurrency is, in part, courtesy of the cryptographic hash function and Merkle trees. Merkle trees put the "fun" in fungible and nonfungible tokens, make the blocks on a blockchain unique, and ensure that smart contracts don't get outsmarted.

A Decentralized World

We're just getting started. Those who have stood on Ralph Merkle's shoulders are about to usher in an era of individualism, privacy, and personal control that we have not seen... um... ever.

It might be fun to unpack the technology from the first paragraph, but let's save that for another time. Instead, let's concentrate on the wireless, trustless, decentralized transaction. When the potential patron gets in range of the door, whatever tech they are using presents a token to the tech the club is using. The token verifies that the potential patron is over the age of 21, but offers no other information. This single data point meets the first condition of the smart contract that controls admission to the club. The potential patron is then automatically asked to tender the cover charge of 5 ADA. ADA are tokens (cryptocurrency) minted on the Cardano blockchain. When the 5 ADA tokens are received by the club's crypto wallet, the final condition of the smart contract is met and the door opens.

With Central Authorities

There are certain things about this transaction that are very familiar. You need to be over 21 to get into a bar, and you have to pay the cover charge (unless you are friends with the bouncer at the door). Yes, you can do this right now with a credit card or any number of other digital tools, but if you did it right now, you'd be leaving a massive data trail. You'd be handing a stranger your driver's license. You would be paying with a credit card that must be cleared by a central authority that already has all of your personal information, plus a profile of everything you've ever done with that credit card. Today, you would be using a smartphone tied to a commercial carrier network, and that carrier not only has all of your personal information but also has aggregated a massive profile of everywhere that phone has been, everyone you've ever called or texted, and all of the data from every data collection opportunity you forgot to opt out of.

Without Central Authorities

Contrast that experience with the trustless, decentralized experience we've posited. Here, the radio in your phone might still be tied to a carrier, but your digital wallet doesn't need internet access to function. It could connect to the club via WiFi or Bluetooth or unlicensed 5G spectrum.

The Return of Privacy

There's even more privacy and data sovereignty to think about. First, no extra data is made available to the club owner. There are only two things the club owner needs to know. Are you over 21? Did you pay the cover charge? In this case, your private, immutable, decentralized ID confirmed that you exceeded the minimum age, without revealing your actual age or anything else about you. Second, it would not matter if one of your friends was running the front of house when you arrived because the funds (in the form of ADA) were immediately and irrevocably transferred from your digital wallet to the club's digital wallet as a condition to open the door and let you in. No cheating! The funds absolutely changed hands.

This is just a thought starter; you can easily take it much further. There could be a Dutch auction for a limited number of NFT tickets to the club. These NFTs (which are, by definition, smart contracts) could have been written to include promotions for the act performing that evening. Loyalty programs could have been created. In practice, if you can think it up, you can write it into a smart contract. Perhaps the NFT would include payment coupons for the two-drink minimum, discounts, or other incentives.

Empowering Individuals Everywhere

Taking this to the next level, imagine a world where you can freely combine your ideas, your social media skills, your social video skills, your business skills, and all the other creative energy that makes you unique and awesome. Then, remove most (or all) of the friction imposed by the central authorities we've been forced to deal with. That future is literally just months away.

The family of technologies that enable decentralization promises to bring us new levels of financial freedom, personal data sovereignty, and a wealth of opportunities.

The Creator Class & NFTs

From a financial perspective, the pandemic hit the creator class hard. With the usual venues for live performances and exhibitions closed, artists, musicians, singers, actors, and creators of every description have been forced to fend for themselves. But something very new (and kind of amazing) happened. The result may be the emergence of a first-time-ever, self-sufficient, profitable creator class.

The stereotype of a "starving artist" is old and hackneyed. Fine artists aren't supposed to care about stuff like food or shelter. They've been "suffering for their art" for centuries. Dancers aren't big eaters, so no one ever thinks about "starving dancers." But musicians haven't fared much better.

Papa Bach was a church organist and an organ repairman on the side. Mozart was always borrowing money from his friends and relatives, although he did make some real money now and again. Beethoven didn't die poor, but he also lived from commission to commission. Prior to 2021, there is one thing that every artist has had in common with every other artist who ever lived: they practiced their art at the pleasure of a patron.

Patrons

Whether it was a monarch, a rich person, a corporation, a media company, a label, a museum, a you-fill-in-the blank, someone with money has funded practically every art project ever. There are a few notable exceptions, of course, but they do not prove the rule. In modern history, the vast majority of artists (no matter the artform) have both wanted and needed the equivalent of a "recording contract with a major label" to eat and pay the rent while attempting to accomplish their artistic goals.

The Mother of Invention

The creator class has undergone one of the most noticeable pandemic-accelerated digital transformations. Visit YouTube or TikTok or Instagram (or any other social video site) and you are sure to find a creator fully empowered with direct-to-consumer (DTC) business tools. From payment processing to analytics to production capabilities, literally everything a creator needs to "get paid" is available with little or no investment. This is more than a digital version of passing the hat to support your busking. There is a massive tech infrastructure emerging to power, enable, and profit symbiotically with the evolving creator class.

After its most recent raise, Patreon (a platform that connects over 200,000 creators with about 7 million fans) was valued at $4 billion (triple its value in September 2020). Cameo is a site that allows celebrities to send personalized videos directly to fans (for a fee, of course). OnlyFans is a favorite app of sex workers and physical fitness experts.

What's important to understand is that every social video post has become an opportunity to promote original content that fans can support, and all of these apps (and dozens of others) are purpose-built to facilitate the remuneration of creators by their fans.

NFTs, Crypto, and the Arts

Have you recently started collecting NFT art? If so, you are in the vanguard of the nascent creator economy.

We're in the middle of the NFT hype-cycle, so it's hard to separate the hucksters and charlatans from

Shelly Palmer

the real opportunities afforded by ERC721 and ERC1155 smart contracts recorded on distributed ledgers. Due to the insane prices of some recent NFT transactions, it seems like everyone who's anyone is getting into the game. Seven-time Super Bowl champion Tom Brady announced he would launch an NFT platform called Autograph in early 2021.

There are many excellent uses for NFTs, especially when it comes to the creator class. One of the biggest issues of our day is the ability for anyone to mash-up anything and call it their own. Take a few measures of music from one song, a beat from another, a sound effect from a favorite movie, a line of dialogue from an amazing video, mash 'em up, and you've got a new (albeit derivative) work. Who gets paid, and how?

Our copyright and intellectual property laws afford protection for creators, but enforcement is extremely difficult. It requires big, centralized organizations such as recorded music companies, publishers, performing rights organizations, movie studios, media companies, and others to monitor, manipulate, and control the granting of rights and the flow of money. NFTs have the potential to decentralize this entire ecosystem.

Said differently, as blockchain technology evolves, transaction speed increases, and transaction fees decrease (all of which are slowly, but surely happening), and as more content becomes uniquely identifiable using NFTs, the need for central authorities (a.k.a. gatekeepers) will diminish and possibly disappear altogether, as the creator class will be able to do it by themselves. The concept of an open, honest, one-to-one relationship between creator and community isn't new, but the technology to do it at scale is.

Nuber: The End of Uber and Central Authority

A study found that drivers were "finding ways to trick the algorithms that Uber uses to control them to cancel fares they didn't want and to avoid the unpopular UberPool" and "organizing mass 'switch-offs' so the lack of drivers in a certain area causes surge pricing."

This should surprise no one. Many Uber drivers feel (rightly or wrongly) that they are underpaid, overworked, and generally treated unfairly. The drivers have tried to unionize, they ad hoc collectively bargain, and they have vigorously campaigned on social media to protest their work conditions.

A Central Authority

At a macro level, these drivers are not unhappy with Uber; they are unhappy being subservient to a central authority. This is not a new story. History is replete with tales of the oppressed proletariat rising up against their aristocratic overlords. Revolts of this type have not, historically speaking, ended well for the noble-born.

The entire Internet is highly centralized. Data are routed through trusted servers on trusted networks. You trust Google with your email. You trust Facebook with your friends. You trust your online banker with your money. You trust Amazon with your credit card and shopping data. You trust Verizon when you access its network. To do business online today is to trust central entities who know everything about you and your actions.

What If There Was No Central Authority?

Here's an idea I'll call "Nuber," a technology that offers all the value Uber offers, but the drivers get all the money. Here's how it would work.

At Nuber, a licensed ride-sharing service driver (an individual with a local business license, a commercial driver's license, and the required insurance) could be summoned through a meta-ride-sharing app and paid directly with no central authority such as Uber or Lyft. There would be no middleman; it would just be you and a licensed, customer-reviewed driver. Nuber would work exactly like

Uber, but all the value captured by Uber would be recaptured by the drivers. Great for drivers, not so great for the central authority, Uber.

Now, apply this idea (a trusted decentralized network) to every type of on-demand business. In this new sharing economy, chatbots, meta-apps, or a simple search would yield a list of accurately reviewed (only by customers who had purchased the goods or services as verified by the underlying technology) vendors in merit order.

Imagine if you had software on your smartphone that would do some quick math to determine which offer was best for you at the moment you were in the market.

How different would the sharing economy be if everything you wanted to share was offered in a real-time auction with no middleman or central authority, if it was purely a free market based on supply and demand?

When Will Nuber Exist?

Blockchain is about to transition from a potentially valuable technology to a revenue-generating one as the hundreds of startups working with blockchain and smart contracts bring their solutions to market.

The only things standing in the way of the new Nuber are a few motivated individuals, a GitHub account, and enough chocolate-covered coffee beans to keep the teams awake while they work on it. This is the whole point; there's basically nothing standing in the way of this new approach to economic equality.

Is this really the end of Uber? Probably not. Nuber is just an idea (and a trademark infringement lawsuit waiting to happen), but it will be exciting to see how trusted, decentralized network technologies change the world.

Gun Sale Background Checks: Blockchain Can Help

The NRA and advocates for gun safety and common sense gun laws found common ground in background checks. Both sides say gun purchasers should face rigorous background checks, which is an excellent starting point for a constructive and productive dialogue.

The majority of Americans agree that background checks make sense. But progress in establishing a system for background checks has been impeded over the years by legacy infrastructure, outdated technology, and policy disagreements about what data should be shared. "Background checks" is an easy concept to communicate, but doing an actual background check is exceptionally complex.

A blockchain-based background check system would offer several benefits over the existing technological infrastructure, including reduced administrative costs, reduced fraud, and increased confidence in the veracity of search results.

The Current System

Today, several databases must be accessed in order to do a federally-compliant background check. A federally-licensed dealer (a person or organization with a Federal Firearms License) must access the National Crime Information Center (NICS) database, the Interstate Identification Index, and the National Instant Criminal Background Check System Index. This is done via telephone or the internet. If there is no match, the sale may proceed.

However, the FBI has three business days to seek additional information (from the judiciary or law enforcement records) to approve or deny a sale. Some states have their own NICS databases. Some states do their own handgun background checks, then pass information to the FBI for rifle and shotgun background checks. If you think this is starting to sound complicated, you're right; there are all kinds of rules and regulations at local, state, and federal levels about how to enter someone into the system and who may be exempted.

How Would Blockchain Help?

If all of this data were available on distributed ledgers, background checks would be more comprehensive and few, if any, transactions would be approved because officials had failed to find any additional data within the three-day time period.

Local, tribal, state, and federal agencies would have to agree to participate, as would law enforcement and the judicial departments. But if they all participated, all of the necessary background data would be encrypted and living in immutable blocks, ready to be searched. A blockchain containing this background check data would be valuable to every security agency.

Why Governments Fear Crypto: A Lesson from Facebook

The Declaration of Independence powerfully describes the idea that a representative government could be established by, and be for, those who would be governed:

We hold these truths to be self-evident, that all men are created equal, that they are endowed by their Creator with certain unalienable Rights, that among these are Life, Liberty and the pursuit of Happiness.—That to secure these rights, Governments are instituted among Men, deriving their just powers from the consent of the governed...

This second paragraph of Thomas Jefferson's historic document is the heart of America's representative democracy, and it clearly separates us from the tyrannical monarchy that inspired our fight for independence.

There are, of course, several other forms of governments. There are lawful monarchies, aristocracies, and timocracies, and corrupt forms of each, such as tyrannies, oligarchies, and anarchy. But all of these forms (regardless of lawfulness or unlawfulness) share at least three fundamental traits: government control of the military, currency, and information.

Is Facebook a Government?

When I think about Facebook and the attributes that empower governments, I can't help but wonder: Is Facebook a government?

With a population of ~3 billion, Facebook is the largest assembly of people in history. Facebook's users are the willing subjects of Mark Zuckerberg, a benevolent monarch who has complete control of what his subjects see and do on Facebook. As far as I can tell, he is a good king whose stated mission is "Give people the power to build community and bring the world closer together."

Zuckerberg became king because he offered his subjects safety, security, and prosperity (in this case, for their digital lives). The people have self-assembled around his mission, and the population of Facebook continues to grow.

Information

Facebook clearly controls the flow of information. Even though the vast majority of "control" is performed by AI, the AI was trained to achieve specific goals. In Facebook's case, the goal is to keep you engaged. The more time you spend on Facebook, the more successful Facebook will be.

The Military

Facebook does not have a physical military (other than whatever armed security Facebook has for its executives), but information has become increasingly weaponized in the past 10 years or so, and Facebook is a high-powered ordnance.

According to Facebook, it is doing everything it can to fight for the good guys. However, if Facebook wanted to become a "bad actor," it is well within its power. (This is the basis of all kinds of global governmental inquiries and a serious source of pain for Facebook.)

Currency

This brings us to currency. Facebook planned a cryptocurrency called Libra and a digital wallet called Calibra. Libra and Calibra would promote financial inclusion for the unbanked and would feature more privacy and decentralization attributes than most critics expected. This long-term vision should not surprise anyone, because Mr. Zuckerberg's complete control of the company empowers him to think long-term.

Libra would have faced a set of significant technical hurdles including speed of transactions, scale, and security, but let's assume that any technical hurdle could be overcome by Facebook's exceptional engineering capabilities. What happens then?

A Monarchy Backed by a Plutocracy

In June 2019, Facebook announced its plans for a cryptocurrency called Libra, a digital wallet called Calibra, and the Libra Association, a supporting plutocracy with a membership fee of $10 million. Founding members got an option to become validator node operators, got a vote on the Libra Council, and earned interest on their investment.

Libra was designed to be stable and would have been backed by deposits of real cash. While the value of these deposits will float by definition (as they are deposits of foreign and domestic fiat currencies), when compared with other cryptocurrencies, Libra would have been rock solid.

The Country of Facebook

Not surprisingly, the U.S. Government forced Facebook to abandon Libra and Calibra, so our democracy is safe for now. But if Facebook had been allowed to launch those two digital products, it would have had control of information (Facebook, WhatsApp, and Instagram), weaponized information (a virtual military), and currency (Libra). I'm pretty sure that would have made Facebook the largest government on earth.

Congress was right to be concerned. If I were the U.S. government (or any government for that matter), I'd wonder if this was the birth of a new form of virtual government, one that was truly opt-in. You can push back and say it's a monarchy supported by an oligarchy and, technically, you'd be right. In practice, though, people are not forced to be citizens of Facebook; they choose to be. It is citizenship by choice. No seeking asylum, no immigration process. You just need a login.

Imagine a government where each geographic area governed itself via direct votes from local mobile devices. Imagine a government where people who had similar interests and beliefs could easily connect, communicate, and self-govern. Imagine... oh, wait. I don't have to imagine anything. This is already how Facebook works. No wonder the representatives elected to our representative democracy were scared out of their wits.

Porn Leads Tech, Again

In September 2021, OnlyFans (OF) announced that—for business reasons—it was going to ban sexually explicit content. Five days later, the company reversed its decision. Upon hearing the original news, millions of users (creators and subscribers) suddenly cried out in terror as they realized that OF was going the way of Tumblr (which is probably why OF revered its decision). At the same time, half the engineers on the planet stopped what they were doing to contemplate how they could rearrange their lives to code an uncensored app to take OF's place. Porn leads tech. It always has, it always will. Which raised the question, what would a successor app look like under the hood? Let's play pretend.

A Direct Copy

By far the easiest thing to do is to build a direct clone of OF and leave it uncensored. This is child's play. Big porn dominates the online porn landscape. (xvideos.com and pornhub.com are the 9th and 10th most popular websites in the world.) It can easily use existing tech to accommodate the creators that OF is abandoning. But wait. What if OF creators don't want to be associated with the porn industry? That's a marketing problem with several easy solutions. The tech is the tech.

A Direct Copy Plus

Another approach would be to do a direct knock-off of the app, but add a token (cryptocurrency) component so that users could anonymously or pseudonymously participate and profit from the value they create. I'm not sure why OF didn't just do this. It would have been a future-thinking approach to solving their problem, and while not a guarantee, trying and failing at a DeFi solution is probably preferable to Tumblr-ing into obscurity. It's easy to imagine a centralized app with an associated centralized cryptocurrency schema that would yield a fungible, freely exchangeable store of value.

A Web 3.0 Solution

This is where it gets interesting. Web 3.0 apps are nontrivially different from Web 2.0 apps (see Web 3.0 Things You Should Know). While there is no agreed-upon definition of Web 3.0, a next-generation Dapp (decentralized app) might include some of the following attributes:

No central servers —by definition, a Dapp (website/app) will be a peer-to-peer application built on a blockchain. So, content will not be "served" from an IP address; content will have an ID and be stored on a plurality of nodes across the network. In theory, this means a successful Dapp with thousands of nodes and millions of users can't be shut down. In practice, the number of users determines the Dapp's fate.

Uncensored content —because there is no central authority, there is no one to censor the content. The community of users could (in theory) set community guidelines, but since this Dapp would be purpose-built, one can assume there would be no mechanism to censor any content. What about child porn, misinformation, hate speech, or other generally banned content? Nope. Uncensored means uncensored.

Immutable content —In theory, content on a Dapp is immutable. Once created, content is given an immutable ID (as opposed to an IP address). In practice, you need to create special workflows to edit and update content. Dynamic content also requires some engineering gymnastics. But these technical hurdles all have workarounds, and the tools get better every day. Can you ever delete content from a peer-to-peer network? No. You can mask it (sort of), but once content is out in the wild, it will live as long as it is available on at least one client/server node.

Self-sovereign identity (SSI) —In theory, users could use some form of SSI schema to limit the data collected by the Dapp. This is a noble goal and one of the areas where porn has led tech in the past. There aren't many people who want their significant others to see "pornhub.com" on their credit card statements. And no one wants to learn that their porn-viewing history and login credentials are available on WikiLeaks.

Utility tokens and a reward system —In theory, creators can become validator nodes in a proof-of-stake (POS) token minting ecosystem and be rewarded with a token for validating transactions on the network. Subscribers could also be validator nodes and could be rewarded for validating transactions or for exhibiting certain behaviors, such as amount of view hours, or help with recruiting new users, etc. The tokens might even be able to be listed on centralized exchanges such as Coinbase, FTX, or Kraken, and even be exchangeable for fiat currencies. In practice, because centralized exchanges are subject to Know Your Customer (KYC) and other business rules, it is unlikely that these tokens would be listed. However, these tokens would be a fungible store of value, and they would be exchangeable for other tokens (cryptocurrencies), including stablecoins, on DEXs (decentralized exchanges).

Will Any of This Happen?

The fate of OnlyFans is still unclear. It may survive and thrive. It may go the way of Tumblr. Time will tell. The important thing here is that there are several different approaches to replacing the void its "business decision" would have created. This was not true two years ago. Back then, any replacement app would have to have been created as a technological copy of OF, and because of the intersection of technology and business rules, any replacement app would have been subject to the same "business reasons" for OF's decision to ban sexually explicit content. This is no longer the case. Any new version of OF can take advantage of a completely new way to create and share value. Will DeFi help porn lead tech once again? History says it will.

Crypto: Parlor Trick or Paradigm Shift?

Technology is meaningless unless it changes the way we behave. As many of you have pointed out, my writing is increasingly focused on blockchain, cryptocurrency, smart contracts and NFTs, decentralized finance (DeFi), Web 3.0, and the role AI and other nascent computational tools may play in the future. There's a simple reason. They are all behavior-changing technologies.

At one end of the spectrum, there's the potential of an alternative, decentralized system for value exchange that challenges our understanding about the role of central governance. At the other end of the spectrum, this is nothing more than a fad which can be easily ignored. In my experience, no technology is ever "either, or."

As you know, almost $8 trillion of wealth vaporized when the dot-com bubble burst in 2000. Those speculative losses didn't have anything to do with the underlying technology; it was all about the hype. With that in mind, think about this...

Crypto Is a Ponzi Scheme

On the surface: Yes. You're absolutely right. If you analyze the tokenomics of almost every cryptocurrency, you will find a scheme of some sort, and it will almost certainly be to the benefit of those who sit at the center of the process. Whether there was an ICO or some other method of minting, allocating, and distributing the original number of tokens (crypto), someone has chosen the initial "big winners" in advance.

Wherever you find information asymmetry, you will find a financial engineer smart enough to take advantage of it (and you).

Under the hood: The tools and techniques used to develop decentralized value exchange systems are fundamental building blocks for the future. Whether or not you choose to use a public or private blockchain – or any blockchain at all – easily explorable, cryptographically hashed distributed ledgers serve a wide range of business use cases. The most important use for the tokens (cryptocurrencies) that reward and empower the users of any DeFi platform is to provide the financial incentives. Crypto and their associated platforms need to be tested and they are worthy of serious study.

Why Use Blockchain when a Secure, Well-structured Database Will Do?

On the surface: Yes. You're absolutely right. This is the most important question you can ask about any potential blockchain project. Most of the time, there is zero reason to use a blockchain. Blockchains are slower and less secure than anyone will admit. They are hard to use. They are terrible places to store large amounts of data. Blockchains have very limited use cases!

Under the hood: We are so used to central authorities imposing rules and regulations on our transactions, it is hard to allow ourselves to think about a world where this is not an immutable law of life. Blockchain technologies (writ large) allow people (or machines) who do not know or trust each other to do business. You trade the security of a central bank or a central government (and their imposed rules, regulations, and costs) for the freedom to do what you like with anyone in the world at any time. This group of technologies is powerful and ubiquitous. Learning how to use them (or learning how others use them) is as fundamentally important as learning any other global IT standard.

NFTs Are a Scam!

On the surface: Yes. You're absolutely right. What is the point of paying to "own" something that everyone else already has a free copy of? It's madness! There's only one *Mona Lisa*. Every other representation of it is clearly a copy. But who in their right mind pays $69,000,000 for a .gif that I can Google and download for free?

Under the hood: NFTs are smart contracts. The technology empowers the creator of the NFT to impose automatic business rules on the initial transaction and all subsequent transactions. Because the results are written to a public blockchain, the chain of custody is accurate and immutable. Can you imagine a business case where (regardless of when, where, or why it occurred) you would benefit from a contract that was automatically executed when the conditions of the contract were met? NFTs and smart contracts don't require a blockchain to function, but coupled with utility tokens or cryptocurrency and a publicly explorable blockchain, they are a new way to do business. Billions of dollars of business have already been transacted using these tools. It is more than worthy of study.

Web 3.0 Is a Crippled Version of Web 2.0. It's All Hype!

On the surface: Yes. You're absolutely right. Web 3.0 websites are clunky and hard to build. When you're done, if you've done a good job, users can't tell if it's a Web 3.0 or 2.0 site because (in success) it looks exactly like a Web 2.0 (current) website. What a waste of time!

Under the hood: There are technical challenges, to be sure. But the progress in the past few years has been remarkable. Big topics: Oracles vs. APIs, Content IDs vs. URLs, decentralized data vs. centralized databases, zero censorship possible vs. imposed government regulations. We all have experience with BitTorrent or other peer-to-peer file systems. They tend to suck. This is different. The ability to financially reward nodes on a Web 3.0 platform creates a way for a community of interest or a community of passion to easily exchange value. This is very clearly a new way to organize global communities. It may never be a way to rebuild the web (I'm not sure the web needs to be rebuilt), but I can rattle off a remarkably long list of potential use cases for every business I work with.

Push Back Hard, but Don't Pretend It's Not Happening

I have no plans to stop thinking about the future. I have no plans to stop exploring what's new, what's next, and what it means for your business – and mine.

Conclusion

Hopefully, you are feeling empowered by your newfound blockchain, smart contract and cryptocurrency knowledge.

These technologies should inspire you to create new and interesting ways to reduce costs, increase margins, and improve productivity.

Please remember the key question:

Why is a blockchain a better solution than a well-structured, secure database?

If you have a good answer, you can start writing the functional specification for your blockchain-powered project.

Shameless plug: If you need help or just want to run your ideas by us, please feel free to contact us at info@shellypalmer.com. We'd love to hear from you.

Blockchain Glossary

Every profession is a conspiracy against the laity, and the world of crypto is no exception. In that spirit, I offer this glossary of terms that will make you sound as if you are completely informed and up-to-date when discussing your next crypto project.

For an up-to-date list of useful links to the decentralized ecosystem (Crypto, NFTs, DeFi, DEX, Blockchain) please visit shellypalmer.com/blockchain.

Tip o' the hat to George Bernard Shaw, Campbell R. Harvey, Ashwin Ramachandran, Joey Santoro, Wikipedia, some friends, and a bunch of subject-specific websites I've visited over the past decade.

Address. The address is the identifier where a transaction is sent. The address is derived from a user's public key, which is derived from the private key by asymmetric key cryptography. In Ethereum, the public key is 512 bits or 128 hexadecimal characters. The public key is hashed (i.e., uniquely represented) with a Keccak-256 algorithm, which transforms it into 256 bits or 64 hexadecimal characters. The last 40 hexadecimal characters are the public key. The public key usually carries the prefix "0x." Also known as public address.

Note: Keccak-256 does not follow the FIPS-202 based standard (a.k.a SHA-3).

Airdrop. A free distribution of tokens into wallets.

AML (Anti-Money Laundering). A regulation designed to detect and report suspicious activity related to illegally concealing the origins of money.

AMM (Automated market maker). An automated market maker (AMM) is a type of decentralized exchange (DEX) protocol that relies on a mathematical formula to price assets. Instead of using an order book like a traditional exchange, assets are priced according to a pricing algorithm. This formula can vary with each protocol.

Asymmetric key cryptography. A cryptographic system that uses pairs of keys: public keys (which may be known to others), and private keys (which may never be known by any except the owner). The generation of such key pairs depends on cryptographic algorithms, which are based on mathematical problems termed one-way functions. Effective security requires keeping the private key private; the public key can be openly distributed without compromising security. See symmetric key cryptography.

Atomic Swap. A smart contract technology that enables the exchange of one cryptocurrency for another without using centralized intermediaries, such as exchanges.

Barter. Usually, the action or system of exchanging goods or services without using money. It is a peer-to-peer exchange mechanism in which two parties agree that goods or services to be exchanged are well-matched. For example, "A" has two pigs and needs a cow. "B" has a cow and needs two pigs.

Bitcoin (BTC). A cryptocurrency invented in 2008 by an unknown person or group of people using the name Satoshi Nakamoto. The currency began use in 2009 when its implementation was released as open-source software.

Blockchain. A decentralized ledger invented in 1991 by Haber and Stornetta. Every node in the ledger has a copy. The ledger can be added to through consensus protocol, but the ledger's history is immutable. The ledger is also visible to anyone.

Bonding curve. A smart contract that allows users to buy or sell a token using a fixed mathematical model. For example, consider a simple linear function in which the token = supply. In this case, the first token would cost 1 ETH and the second token 2 ETH, thereby rewarding early participants. It is possible to have different bonding curves for buying and selling. A common functional form is a logistic curve.

Bricked funds. Funds trapped in a smart contract due to a bug in the contract.

Burn. The removal of a token from circulation, thereby reducing the supply of the token. Burning is achieved by sending the token to an unowned Ethereum address or to a contract incapable of spending. Burning is an important part of many smart contracts. Burning occurs when someone exits a pool and redeems the underlying assets.

Collateralized currency. Paper currency backed by collateral such as gold, silver, or other assets.

Collateralized debt obligation. In traditional finance, this represents a debt instrument such as a mortgage. In DeFI, an example would be a stablecoin overcollateralized with a cryptoasset.

Consensus protocol. The mechanism whereby parties agree to add a new block to the existing blockchain. Both Ethereum and Bitcoin use proof of work, but many other mechanisms exist, such as proof of stake.

Contract account. A type of account in Ethereum controlled by a smart contract.

Credit delegation. A feature whereby users can allocate collateral to potential borrowers who can use the collateral to borrow the desired asset.

Cryptocurrency. A digital token cryptographically secured and transferred using blockchain technology. Leading examples are Bitcoin and Ethereum. Many different types of cryptocurrencies exist, such as stablecoin and tokens that represent digital and non-digital assets.

Cryptographic hash. (a.k.a. "Hash") A one-way function that uniquely represents the input data. It can be thought of as a unique digital fingerprint. The output is a fixed size even though the input can be arbitrarily large. A hash is not encryption because it does not allow recovery of the original message. A popular hashing algorithm is the SHA-256, which returns 256 bits or 64 hexadecimal characters. The bitcoin blockchain uses the SHA-256. Ethereum uses the Keccak-256.

DAO (Decentralized autonomous organization). An algorithmic organization that has a set of rules encoded in a smart contract that stipulates who can execute what behavior or upgrade. A DAO commonly includes a governance token.

Dapp (Decentralized application). Peer-to-peer, permissionless, censorship-resistant applications. Anyone can use them. No central organization controls them.

DeFi (Decentralized finance). A financial infrastructure that does not rely on a centralized institution, such as a bank. Exchange, lending, borrowing, and trading are conducted on a peer-to-peer basis using blockchain technology and smart contracts.

Defi Legos. The idea that combining protocols to build a new protocol is possible. Sometimes referred to as DeFi Money Legos or composability. DEX. See decentralized exchange.

DEX (Decentralized exchange). A platform that facilitates token swaps in a noncustodial fashion. The two mechanisms for DEX liquidity are order book matching and AMM.

Digest. See cryptographic hash. Also known as message digest.

Direct incentive. A payment or fee associated with a specific user action intended to be a reward for positive behavior. For example, suppose a collateralized debt obligation becomes undercollateralized. The condition does not automatically trigger liquidation. An external-ly-owned account must trigger the liquidation, and a reward (direct incentive) is given for triggering the liquation.

Double spend. A problem that plagued digital currency initiatives in the 1980s and 1990s: perfect copies can be made of a digital asset, so it can be spent multiple times. The Satoshi Nakamoto white paper in 2008 solved this problem using a combination of blockchain technology and proof of work.

Equity token. A type of cryptocurrency that represents ownership of an underlying asset or a pool of assets.

EOA (Externally owned account). An Ethereum account controlled by a specific user.

ERC-20. Ethereum Request for Comments (ERC) related to defining the interface for fungible tokens. Fungible tokens are identical in utility and functionality. The U.S. dollar is fungible currency in that all $20 bills are identical in value and twenty $1 bills are equal to the $20 bill.

ERC-721. Ethereum Request for Comments (ERC) related to defining the interface for nonfungible tokens. Nonfungible tokens are unique and are often used for collectibles or specific assets, such as a loan.

ERC-1155. Ethereum Request for Comments (ERC) related to defining a multi-token model in which a contract can hold balances of a number of tokens, either fungible or non-fungible.

Ether (ETH). Ethereum's cryptocurrency.

Ethereum. Second-largest cryptocurrency blockchain, which has existed since 2015. The currency is known as ether (ETH). Ethereum has the ability to run computer programs known as smart contracts. Ethereum is considered a distributed computational platform.

Ethereum 2.0. A proposed improvement on the Ethereum blockchain that uses horizontal scaling and proof of stake consensus.

Faucet. A smart contract that mints "test ETH" (a valueless version of Ethereum's cryptocurrency) for use on a Testnet.

Fiat currency. Uncollateralized paper currency (essentially an IOU from a government).

Fintech (Financial Technology). A general term that refers to technological advances in finance. It broadly includes technologies in the payments, trading, borrowing, and lending spaces. Fintech often includes big data and machine learning applications.

Flash loan. An uncollateralized loan with zero counterparty risk and zero duration. Used to facilitate arbitrage or to refinance a loan without pledging collateral. Has no counterparty risk because in a single transaction: the loan is created, all buying and selling using the loan funding is completed, and the loan is paid in full.

Flash swap. Feature of some DeFi protocols whereby a contract sends tokens before the user pays for them with assets on the other side of the pair. Allows for near-instantaneous arbitrage. Whereas a flash loan must be repaid with the same asset, a flash swap allows the flexibility of repaying with a different asset. A key feature is that all trades occur within a single Ethereum transaction.

Fork. In the context of open source code, an upgrade or enhancement to an existing protocol that connects to the protocol's history. A user has the choice of using the old or the new protocol. If the new protocol is better and attracts sufficient mining power, it will win. Forking is a key mechanism to assure efficiency in DeFi.

Gas (a.k.a. Gas Prices or Gas Fees). A fee required to execute a transaction and to execute a smart contract. Gas is the mechanism that allows Ethereum to deal with the halting problem.

Geoblock. Technology that blocks users from certain countries bound by regulation that precludes the application.

Governance token. The right of an owner to vote on changes to the protocol. Examples include the MakerDAO MKR token and the Compound COMP token.

Gwei (gigawei). 1,000,000,000 wei. Wei, the smallest (base) unit of ether (ETH), is what Sats (a.k.a. satoshi) are to bitcoin (BTC).

Halting problem. A computer program in an infinite loop. Ethereum solves this problem by requiring a fee for a certain amount of computing. If the gas is exhausted, the program stops.

Hash. See cryptographic hash.

Hexadecimal. A counting system in base-16 that includes the first 10 numbers (0 through 9) plus the first six letters of the alphabet (a through f). Each hexadecimal character represents 4 bits, where 0 is 0000 and the 16th (f) is 1111.

Horizontal scaling. An approach that divides the work of the system into multiple pieces, retaining decentralization but increasing the throughput of the system through parallelization. This is also known as sharding. Ethereum 2.0 takes this approach in combination with a proof of stake consensus algorithm.

IDO (Initial DeFi Offering). A method of setting an initial exchange rate for a new token. A user can be the first liquidity provider on a pair (such as the new token and a stablecoin, like USDC). Essentially, the user establishes an artificial floor for the price of the new token.

Shelly Palmer

Impermanent loss. Applies to AMM, where a contract holds assets on both sides of a trading pair. Suppose the AMM imposes a fixed exchange ratio between the two assets, and both assets appreciate in market value. The first asset appreciates by more than the second asset. Users drain the first asset, and the contract is left holding only the second asset. The impermanent loss is the value of the contract if no exchange took place (value of both tokens) minus the value of the contract after it was drained (value of second token).

Incentive. A broad term used to reward productive behavior. Examples include direct incentives and staked incentives.

Keeper. A class of externally owned accounts that is an incentive to perform an action in a DeFi protocol of a Dapp. The keeper receives a reward in the form of a flat fee or a percentage of the incented action. For example, the keeper receives a fee for liquidating a collateralized debt obligation when it becomes undercollateralized.

KYC (Know Your Customer). A provision of U.S. regulation common to financial services regulation requiring users to identify themselves, which hasled to geoblocking of U.S. customers from certain DEX functionalities.

Layer 2. A scaling solution built on top of a blockchain that uses cryptography and economic guarantees to maintain desired levels of security. For example, small transactions can occur using a multi-signature payment channel. The blockchain is only used when funds are added to the channel or withdrawn.

Liquidity provider (LP). A user that earns a return by depositing assets into a pool or a smart contract.

Mainnet. The fully-operational production blockchain behind a token, such as the Bitcoin blockchain or the Ethereum blockchain. Often used to contrast with testnet.

Miner. Miners cycle through various values of a nonce to try to find a rare hash value in a proof of work blockchain. A miner gathers candidate transactions for a new block, adds a piece of data called a nonce, and executes a cryptographic hashing function. The nonce is varied and the hashing continues. If the miner "wins" by finding a hash value that is very small, the miner receives a direct reward in newly minted cryptocurrency. A miner also earns an indirect reward, collecting fees for the transactions included in their block.

Miner extractable value. The profit derived by a miner. For example, the miner could front run a pending transaction they believe will increase the price of the cryptocurrency (e.g. a large buy).

Shelly Palmer

Mint. An action that increases the supply of tokens. The opposite of burn. Minting often occurs when a user enters a pool and acquires an ownership share. Minting and burning are essential parts of noncollateralized stablecoin models (i.e. when stablecoin gets too expensive more are minted, which increases supply and reduces prices). Minting is also a means to reward user behavior. You mint NFTs and cryptocurriences created in many Layer 2 solutions.

Networked liquidity. The idea that any exchange application can lever the liquidity and rates of any other exchange on the same blockchain.

Node. A computer on a network that has a full copy of a blockchain.

Nonce (Number Only Once). A counter mechanism for miners as they cycle through various values when trying to discover a rare cryptographic hash value.

NFT (Non-fungible token). As defined by ERC-721 and ERC-1155, a unique token often used for collectibles or specific assets, such as a loan.

On chain. Slang term used to describe transactions reflected on a blockchain.

Optimistic rollup. A scaling solution whereby transactions are aggregated off-chain into a single digest that is submitted to the chain on a periodic basis.

Oracle. A method whereby information is gathered outside of a blockchain. Parties must agree on the source of the information.

Order book matching. A process in which all parties must agree on the swap exchange rate. Market makers can post bids and asks to a DEX and allow takers to fill the quotes at the pre-agreed price. Until the offer is taken, the market maker has the right to withdraw the offer or update the exchange rate.

Perpetual futures contract. Similar to a traditional futures contract, but without an expiration date.

Proof of stake (PoS). An alternative consensus mechanism and a key feature of Ethereum 2.0, wherein the staking of an asset on the next block replaces the mining of blocks as in proof of work. In proof of work, miners need to spend on electricity and equipment to win a block. In proof of stake, validators commit some capital (the stake) to attest that the block is valid. Validators make themselves available by staking their cryptocurrency and are randomly selected to propose a block, which needs to be attested by a majority of the other validators. Validators profit by both proposing a block as well as attesting to the validity of others' proposed blocks. If a validator acts maliciously, there is a penalty mechanism whereby their stake is slashed.

Proof of work (PoW). Originally advocated by Back in 2002, the consensus mechanism for the two leading blockchains: Bitcoin and Ethereum. Miners compete to find a hash, which is hard to find but easy to verify. Miners are rewarded for finding the cryptographic hash and using it to add a block to the blockchain. The computing difficulty of finding the hash makes it impractical to go backward to rewrite the history of a leading blockchain.

Router contracts. In the context of DEX, contracts that determine the most efficient path of swaps in order to get the lowest slippage, if no direct trading pair is available (e.g. on Uniswap).

SATS – Satoshis. The smallest denomination of a Bitcoin (a hundreth of a millionth, or 0.00000001 BTC).

Satoshi Nakamoto. The name used by the presumed pseudonymous person or persons who developed bitcoin, authored the bitcoin white paper, and created and deployed bitcoin's original reference implementation. As part of the implementation, Nakamoto also devised the first blockchain database.

Scaling risk. The limited ability of most current blockchains to handle a larger number of transactions per second. See vertical scaling and horizontal scaling.

Schelling-point oracle. A type of oracle that relies on the owners of a fixed supply of tokens to vote on the outcome of an event or report a price of an asset.

Sharding. Sometimes called horizontal scaling, sharding divides the work of the system into multiple pieces, retaining decentralization but increasing the throughput of the system through parallelization. Ethereum 2.0 takes this approach with the goal of reducing network congestion and increasing the number of transactions per second.

Slashing. A mechanism in proof of stake blockchain protocols intended to discourage certain user misbehavior.

Slashing condition. The mechanism that triggers a slashing. An example of a slashing condition is when under-collateralization triggers a liquidation.

Smart contract. A computer program or transaction protocol that automatically executes when conditions of the agreement are met. The key mechanism for DeFi and Dapps. An important feature of the Ethereum blockchain.

Specie. Metallic currency such as gold or silver (or nickel and copper) that has value on its own (i.e. if melted and sold as a metal).

Stablecoin. A token tied to the value of an asset, such as the U.S. dollar. A stablecoin can be collateralized with physical assets (e.g. the U.S. dollar in USDC) or digital assets (e.g. DAI) or can be uncollateralized (e.g. AMPL and ESD).

Staking. The escrows of funds in a smart contract by a user who is subject to a penalty (slashed funds) if they deviate from expected behavior.

Staked incentive. A token balance held by a smart contract whose purpose is to influence user behavior. A staking reward is designed to encourage positive behavior by giving the user a bonus in their token balance based on the stake size. A staking penalty (slashing) is designed to discourage negative behavior by removing a portion of a user's token balance based on the stake size.

Swap. The exchange of one token for another. In DeFi, swaps are atomic and noncustodial. Funds can be custodied in a smart contract with withdrawal rights exercisable at any time before the swap is completed. If the swap is not completed, all parties retain their custodied funds.

Symmetric key cryptography. A type of cryptography in which a common key is used to encrypt and decrypt a message.

Testnet. An identically functioning blockchain to a mainnet whose purpose is to test software. The tokens associated with the testnet when testing Ethereum, for example, are called test ETH. Test ETH are obtained for free from a smart contract that mints the test ETH (known as a faucet).

Transparency. The ability for anyone to see the code and all transactions sent to a smart contract. A commonly used blockchain explorer is etherscan.io.

Utility token. A fungible token required to utilize some functionality of a smart contract system or with an intrinsic value defined by its respective smart contract system. For example, a stablecoin (whether collateralized or algorithmic) is a utility token.

Vampirism. An exact or near-exact copy of a DeFi platform designed to take liquidity away from an existing platform, often by offering users direct incentives.

Vault. A smart contract that escrows collateral and keeps track of the value of the collateral.

Vertical scaling. The centralization of all

transaction processing to a single large machine, which reduces the communication overhead (transaction/block latency) associated with a proof of work blockchain, such as Ethereum, but results in a centralized architecture in which one machine is responsible for a majority of the system's processing.

Yield farming. A means to provide contract-funded rewards to users for staking capital or using a protocol.

About The Author

Shelly Palmer is a business advisor and technology consultant. He helps Fortune 500 companies with digital transformation, media and marketing. Named LinkedIn's Top Voice in Technology, he is the host of the Shelly Palmer #CryptoWednesday livestream and co-host of Techstream with Shelly Palmer & Seth Everett. He covers tech and business for Good Day New York, writes a weekly column for Adweek, is a regular commentator on CNN and CNBC, and writes a popular daily business blog. Follow @shellypalmer or visit shellypalmer. com.

Resources

The blockchain ecosystem is evolving rapidly.

For the latest information and useful links to the decentralized ecosystem (Crypto, NFTs, DeFi, DEX, Blockchain), please visit:

shellypalmer.com/blockchain

Links

Links referenced in this book can be found at:

shellypalmer.com/blockchain-book-links

Made in the USA
Las Vegas, NV
16 October 2021